EVE

WHAT *Really* HAPPENED IN THE *Garden*

JOYCE TILNEY

Eve, What Really Happened in the Garden?
© 2020 by Joyce Tilney. All Rights Reserved

No part of this publication may be reproduced, stored in a retrieval system, or be transmitted in any form, or by any means, electronic, mechanical, photocopying or otherwise without the prior written consent of the author, Joyce Tilney, or the publisher, Women of God Ministries, Inc. Printed in the Unites States of America

ISBN: 978-0-578-72897-1

Published by Women of God Ministries—joycetilney.com

Cover Design & Interior Formatting: wendywalters.com

Unless otherwise indicated, Scripture quotations are taken from the New King James Version of the Bible. Copyright © 1982 by Thomas Nelson. Used by permission. All rights reserved.

Scriptures marked NLT are taken from the Holy Bible, New Living Translation. Copyright © 1996, 2004. Used by permission of Tyndale House Publishers, Inc., Wheaton, IL 60188. All rights reserved.

Scriptures marked TPT are taken from The Passion Translation of the Bible. Copyright © 2017 by BroadStreet Publishing Group. Used by permission. All rights reserved. thePassionTranslation.com

Scriptures marked NIV are taken from the Holy Bible, New International Version. Copyright © 1973, 1978, 1984, 2011 by Biblica, Inc. Used by permission. All rights reserved worldwide.

The Scripture marked NASB is taken from the New American Standard Bible. Copyright © 1960, 1962, 1963, 1968, 1971, 1972, 1973, 1975, 1977, 1995 by the Lockman Foundation.

The Scriptures marked KJV are taken from the King James Version of the Bible.

To contact the author:

JOYCETILNEY.COM | woman20-eve@yahoo.com

ENDORSEMENTS

I have known Joyce Tilney and her husband Bill for years. When Joyce asked me to review her book, I expected it to be a good read with great incites from the Word of God. I was not disappointed.

Whenever I read a biblical teaching book, I have several criteria for recommending it. First, it must be scripturally accurate. Second, it needs to create in me a greater hunger for God and build faith. Third, it must challenge me—and if need be correct me, without condemning me. This book meets my criteria for a good read. It is full of grace and truth.

I found the theme of Eve in the garden to be refreshing, because I usually have approached the garden story from Adam's viewpoint. I love Joyce's statement that "all sin begins with believing a lie." I love the reference to Eve as the "First Lady of the Garden." To think—Eve was in a perfect location physically, but still fell into sin because she believed a lie.

One of the great messages of this book is that there's life and hope after our mistakes. God doesn't disown us when we fall, because He is always for us not against us. There is mercy and forgiveness at redemption. The theme of putting God's Word first can never be overemphasized. The Word in this book will strengthen your faith.

REV. WOODY WOODSON
Woodson Ministries

In order to embrace the new thing that God is doing on the earth today, the Church often has to go backward before we can move forward. This is to restore truths from Scripture that will help us to walk in God's original intent for us.

In her new book, Joyce Tilney shines a spotlight on the immense value of the Word of God and encourages readers to take God's words to heart in their daily, personal walks of faith.

By focusing on biblically sound foundations, she emphasizes the identity and authority that God has called all believers to step into as co-heirs with Christ. This book will spur you on to "shape the Garden of your life" with words and actions that advance God's Kingdom!

DR. CHÉ AHN
Founder and President, Harvest International Ministry
Founding and Senior Pastor, Harvest Rock Church, Pasadena, CA
International Chancellor, Wagner University
Founder, Ché Ahn Ministries

God brought Joyce into my life at a time when I needed nourishment and encouragement from God's truths. Like many pastor's wives, I had found myself in a lonely place where I was in need of someone to speak into my life. Her teachings from the testimonies of those who have gone before us, as well as her own testimonies, replenished me.

Joyce, once again, you have brought forth profound truth in a simplistic, understandable, yet powerful way from the testimony of Eve and life in the garden! You have given new seeds to plant from the truths of God's Word and shown me areas in my own life where weeds still need to be pulled out in order to make me more like Jesus!

This book will not only bring encouragement in your walk with God, but it will challenge you to build your life on the sure foundation of God's Word, to speak forth words that are in agreement with His Words, and to make choices accordingly. As you do this, you will be a Godly influence on those whom God brings into your midst for His glory, honor and praise! You will want to keep this book in your possession in order to reread it again and again reminding you of these godly principles.

HELEN LEVENGOOD
Hopewell Community Church
RV's on a Mission

In Joyce's new book, *Eve*, she identifies the primary issue that created the events that resulted in Adam and Eve leaving the garden.

This issue has haunted man through the centuries even to this day. Joyce follows this issue through other biblical stories, characters and scripture references. After each chapter is a list of the major points brought to light and is a good plumb line for self-evaluation.

Days after reading *Eve*, I found myself in different situations and choices asking myself if I was following in Eve's footsteps. Reading

Eve will motivate you to examine your obedience to our Heavenly Father. I recommend this book for individuals, group studies and book club.

DR. CAROLYN DRIVER
The Driver Institute of Leadership and Education
www.dilega.com

I met Joyce and her husband, Bill, when they lived in Scotland. She is a gifted teacher and has a passion for the Word of God.

I love the way Joyce brings the reader from Eve's downfall to a wonderful crescendo of creating the brilliant garden of our own life. She reminds us after receiving Jesus as our Lord and Saviour, God restores all that was lost in the Garden.

We must make a choice day by day to consistently and purposefully value God's Word, living each day intentionally choosing to follow the Lord in faith creating our life's Garden to beauty and power – to God's glory!

This is a transformational book to be valued bringing hope that our defeat can be turned to expectation and joy through believing the mighty Word of God. This book would be wonderful for a group Bible Study, meditating on the Scriptures and the Points to Ponder at the end of each chapter.

ANITA MCAULAY
Greenock, Scotland
Self Help Talks…helping you to help yourself through the Word of God.
www.selfhelptalks.com

DEDICATION

This book is dedicated to my four granddaughters:

SAMANTHA TUCKER

HEATHER ALLEN

KAYLA ALLEN

JESSICA TILNEY

Four unique Women of God! You are a joy to my heart! Life is about generations. There is nothing greater than to be blessed by your children's children. What a blessing to my heart to see you all grow into the Women of God that you were created to be! I have seen the joy of your heart, and tears from the sorrow of your heart. You have handled life with dignity that only a strong woman of God can do! You have so much to look forward to as you continue to plant your Garden of Life and continue the generations to come. You put a smile on my face!

ACKNOWLEDGMENTS

A friend in the Lord is a joy in the heart! I have been blessed with friends that God has sent into my life. I value each one and appreciate the encouragement, the help and yes, the corrections that they have brought to my life. I have been enriched in my walk with the Lord with people who speak "the truth," even though it may hurt for a season, but has kept me in my life pursuit of serving the Lord.

My husband, Bill, my best friend on earth listening to my frustration and helping me, "see the light!" I am thankful for his encouragement and the freedom to follow the Lord in the calling to teach the Word of God. Yes, even his red pen! I think he enjoys marking up my articles and manuscripts too much. Without Jesus and Bill Tilney, I am nothing!

My son, Bill, Jr., for his encouragement and help when I am feeling maybe it is time for me to bring out the rocking chair and let someone else do it. His words, "Mom, practice what you preach, there is no age in the spirit, and you are still breathing!" Ouch, I just smile, repent, and say, "let's do it!"

Pat Richardson, a friend in the Lord that I met in Bible School. We have gone our separate ways after graduation, but I always knew that I could call her for prayer. There is no distance in the spirit and some of my richest resources are with friends that I rarely meet in the physical, but always connected in the spirit. Her truthful input reading this book, helped me keep my focus and complete the work.

CONTENTS

13	INTRODUCTION	
19	CHAPTER 1	EVE—THE *First Lady* OF THE *Garden*
25	CHAPTER 2	THE *Value* OF *God's Word*
33	CHAPTER 3	THE *Power* OF THE *Word* OF *God*
39	CHAPTER 4	THE *Power* OF YOUR *Words*
51	CHAPTER 5	EMBRACING *God's Word*
67	CHAPTER 6	*Plant* YOUR OWN *Garden*
77	CHAPTER 7	*You* WERE *Created* FOR *More*
85	CHAPTER 8	AND *God Said ...*
93	CHAPTER 9	IN *Due* SEASON
101	ABOUT THE AUTHOR	MEET *Joyce Tilney*
102	RESOURCES	

INTRODUCTION

"Whatever was written beforehand is meant to instruct us in how to live. The Scriptures impart to us encouragement and inspiration so that we can live in hope and endure all things."
ROMANS 15:4 TPT

The Lord spoke to my heart as I was traveling through the beautiful highlands of Scotland, "Teach women today from women of yesterday." He then confirmed that word with the above Scripture.

At the time I really did not realize the wisdom and the significance of the Scripture regarding my ministry. I began to study the women in the Bible and was delighted as the Holy Spirit began to give revelation to me regarding these women and the prophetic power of the testimony of their lives.

God has given us real life testimonies in the Bible as examples to help build our trust in Him and to understand how He worked with men and women in the earth.

These are not just "Bible stories," but testimonies of how God worked through the lives of men and women in their lifetime. As the Scriptures stated, they are to instruct us in how to live in hope and endure all things.

We hear so much about "Bible stories" for bedtime and for children, we often do not understand the significance and purpose of the testimonies in the Word of God and how they relate to our daily walk with the Lord.

Psalm 119:111 tells us, "Your testimonies I have taken as a heritage forever, for they *are* the rejoicing of my heart." This is our inheritance and our "family history!" Testimonies give us God's perspective and His version of history, imparting insight and reality from His point of view!

Meditating on the testimonies is a training ground for renewing our minds. The prophetic anointing carried through testimonies brings encouragement and comfort in our time of need giving us that quiet assurance that all things are possible with God!

The testimonies of God's faithfulness to His people impart hope and trust in Him. We learn from their mistakes and their victories! So open your heart as you study the testimonies of God's people. Just as He did for those who walked before us, He will reveal to our spirit the way of escape. He will also give us creative ideas to bring His Kingdom to this earth through you and me as we walk the runway of life.

God blessed Women of God Ministries and opened doors around the world for me to go and minister. I found the heart of women does not change from culture to culture or from century to century. Women's needs are the same throughout the ages. They need to belong, to love and be loved! To find their identity, develop their gifts, maintain a good attitude, juggle responsibilities and learn to forgive and accept forgiveness.

- Sarah told her husband what to do, then got mad at him because he did it!
- Eve had everything a woman could want but was not content.
- Leah, betrayed by her father, rejected by her husband and hated by her sister, learned to walk through the trials of life to a place of honor.

I can relate to these women!

Who are these women from yesterday? Remarkable, real people with real feelings and real struggles! They encountered life head-on. Some walked with God, some disobeyed God! We can learn from both.

We are bombarded today by the views of the world as to who a woman is to be and her place in society. There is only one source of power that can stand against the pressure of society—the power of the Holy Spirit. True womanhood is measured by a woman's own character developed from the Word of God.

Women were born to influence! Did Eve have influence in the Garden? It is particularly important that you, woman of God, understand the beginning of mankind. You are not an afterthought! You were in the heart and mind of God long before you were created.

> **YOU WERE IN THE HEART AND MIND OF GOD LONG BEFORE YOU WERE CREATED**

"So God created man in His *own* image; in the image of God He created him; male and female He created them. Then God blessed them, and God said to them, "Be fruitful and multiply; fill the earth and subdue it; have dominion over the fish of the sea, over the birds of the air, and over every living thing that moves on the earth" (Genesis 1:27-28). When you were born again and became a child of God, God restored the blessing of Eden to you and gave you the same commission as He gave to Adam and Eve. *It is your time in the Garden of Life!*

We must learn to live in this world as a new creation in Christ Jesus. Galatians 6:16 NLT says, "May God's peace and mercy be upon all who live by this principle: they are new people of God." It is a lifelong journey, and I look forward to learning from Eve. What really happened in the Garden of Eden?

I believe the Holy Spirit is going to give us revelation and open the eyes of our understanding so that we can live in the abundance of righteousness, joy and peace as we have been ordained to do in this earth.

It all started in the Garden and we must learn the lessons from the Garden to build our Garden of Life in this world!

*This is not a book about what happened in the Garden. It is a book about **why** it happened!*

Let us get ready to dig up some weeds and plant new seeds!

JOYCE TILNEY
Women of God Ministries

"Nothing stamped with the Divine image and likeness was sent in the world to be trodden on."
ABRAHAM LINCOLN

CHAPTER 1

EVE—THE *First Lady* OF THE *Garden*

*"And Adam called his wife's name Eve,
because she was the mother of all living."*
GENESIS 3:20

If ever a woman had everything going her way it was Eve! She had a perfect husband and a perfect home with no dust and no dirty clothes to pick up! She was the first woman, first wife and first grandmother. It appears that she had it all together.

As we reflect on Eve in the Garden, her fall and her redemption, open your heart and ask the Holy Spirit to open the eyes of your understanding and encourage you from the life of Eve, the first Lady of the Garden.

Eve had the privilege of being there in the beginning. God had created the world in which Eve lived. Everything was beautiful. The air was fresh, and the water was pure. All of creation lived in harmony. Her marriage was perfect, and her relationship with God was a joy.

Adam and Eve had been created in the image of God! They had dominion over all things including every creeping thing that crawls on the earth. God blessed them and told them (male and female) to be fruitful and multiply.

He also gave them specific instructions when He placed them in the Garden of Eden. "And the LORD God commanded the man, saying, 'Of every tree of the garden you may freely eat; but of the tree of the knowledge of good and evil you shall not eat, *for in the day that you eat of it you shall surely die*'" (Genesis 2:16-17).

God did not prohibit Adam and Eve from interacting with any part of His creation, except one tree. He had given Adam and Eve a free will and the ability to make choices. They had a choice to make about this tree. God did not want them eating its fruit because He did not want them to have the knowledge of evil. At this point all they knew was good. God wanted to spare them from evil, just as He desires to do the same for us today.

It happened one day! Satan approached Eve and planted a thought in her mind. "Has God indeed said, 'You shall not eat of every tree of the garden'?" (Genesis 3:1).

Eve responded, "And the woman said to the serpent, "We may eat the fruit of the trees of the garden; but of the fruit of the tree which is in the midst of the garden, God has said, 'You shall not eat it, nor shall you touch it, lest you die'" (Genesis 3:2-3).

Then the serpent said to the woman, "You will not surely die" (Genesis 3:4). This was a lie! God had said, *"You shall surely die"* (Genesis 2:17). *All sin starts with a lie!*

By the words of her mouth Eve traded the eternal for the temporary, the truth for a lie. Satan has one trick—deception. He always includes a little truth with his lie. It worked so well on Eve that he is still using it today to turn our eyes from God's Word.

The fruit was not the problem. Eating the fruit was evidence of what was in her heart. She had chosen to believe satan's word over God's Word. *The temptation was to doubt God's Word!*

We can see by her response to satan, when she added her own words, "nor shall you touch it," that deception had already entered her heart. Words always reveal what is in our heart.

THE TEMPTATION WAS TO DOUBT GOD'S WORD!

As I read and meditated on the life of Adam and Eve in the Garden, I was trying to understand, how could this happen? Everything was perfect. How could you entertain a thought of anything else? I said, "God, what really happened in the Garden?" He immediately dropped in my heart, *"Eve did not value My Word."*

I began to ponder those words spoken to me by the Lord. I felt a warning as I considered the Word of God. I questioned myself, "Do I value the Word of God? Do I understand the importance of

His Word in my daily life? Do I understand the importance of the words I speak?"

After many years, these words still burn in my heart. I still meditate on them and ask the Holy Spirit to guard my heart. Only the truth of God's Word can expose deception.

I urge you to read, meditate and study God's Word. It gives life to those who find it and health to their flesh. (See Proverbs 4:20-23)

It is important that as a Christian, born again by the Spirit of the living God, that we understand the beginning of mankind. When you said yes to Jesus and asked Him to be your Saviour, in a blink of an eye you were translated from the dominion of darkness to the Kingdom of Light. Your eternal destiny was changed because you believed God's Word, came into agreement with the Word of God and spoke it from your heart.

You were "born again" and became a "new creation" in Christ Jesus. Just like Eve, you were created in His image and you are being formed into His likeness. The "forming" is a lifelong process as you grow in the Word of God, which is the Word of Life.

The moment you were born again, God restored the Blessing of Eden to you and gave you the same commission He first gave Adam and Eve in the Garden: to exercise dominion, subdue what needs to be subdued and to be fruitful and multiply and replenish the earth. (Genesis 1:28) To "replenish" means to renew and supply. That is our job as a child of God to continually bring the "good news" of Jesus Christ and become strong in spirit, filled with wisdom and the grace of God.

Whatever happens in this world, whether it's the economy, politics or natural disasters, we have been commissioned to speak God's Word and say, let there be light, in every situation we face in this world.

> *"For God so loved the world that He gave His only begotten Son, that whoever believes in Him should not perish but have everlasting life."*
> JOHN 3:16

POINTS TO PONDER

Study Genesis Chapters 1-5.

- Adam and Eve were created in the image of God according to the likeness of God.

- When you were born again, you became a new creation in Christ Jesus, and you are being formed into His likeness as you grow in the Word of God and walk through the trials of life.

- Eve's temptation was to doubt God's Word.

- Eve did not value the Word of God.

- All sin starts with a lie!

- Your temptation is the same. Do you really believe and trust God to meet all your needs? (Philippians 4:19)

- It is your time in the Garden of life!

- It is time to pull some weeds and plant new seeds!

CHAPTER 2

THE *Value* OF *God's Word*

> *"Every Scripture has been inspired by the Holy Spirit, the breath of God. It will empower you by its instruction and correction, giving you the strength to take the right direction and lead you deeper into the path of godliness. Then you will be God's servant, fully mature and perfectly prepared to fulfill any assignment God gives you."*
> 2 TIMOTHY 3:16-17 TPT

Today just about every family has a Bible at home. Many have several Bibles, different versions of the written Word, and we carry them on our phones and devices. We can have an app that tells us what to read, and then check it off our to do list.

I remember a trip to Hong Kong. A young woman asked me if she could have a page from my Bible. I handed her my Bible. She was overwhelmed to have her own Bible. She held it tightly and wept, promising me she would read it every day. *She valued the Word of God.*

A major concern regarding today's church is that we have lost our love for God's Word. Trying to keep up with all of the aspects of Christian life today can be overwhelming. There are relationships inside and outside of our immediate families and our work and community involvement. On top of this, we have personal Bible study, prayer, fasting, evangelism and mission trips!

So how do we keep all these balls in the air? One lesson I learned in life was to say NO without feeling guilty. We don't have to go along with the crowd!

We must determine our personal values and set boundaries. We need a divine flow in our life. God is first, family is second and everything else flows from that. We must live intentionally on purpose, and as a born-again believer my purpose in life is to know God!

Paul assured Timothy in 2 Timothy 3:16-17 that the source of Scripture is God breathed. It is His Word and carries with it His authority. He then spelled out its purpose and value. The Word of God is profitable for several things: doctrine, reproof, correction and instruction in righteousness. Living in this world, we all need reproof and correction continually to keep our hearts right and open to hear His voice.

Paul then shares the overriding purpose for Scriptures: "…that the man of God may be complete, equipped for every good work." (v. 17) I believe Paul was telling Timothy if he neglected to study God's Word, his life would be incomplete. He would be missing out on a treasury of truth that would give him righteousness, peace and joy that would carry him through all the pitfalls of life.

Look at Adam and Eve. Life was good, they had fellowship with the Lord and all of their needs were met. They had purpose in life to be fruitful and multiply, but suddenly it all changed! They became afraid and independent, trying to meet their own need by sewing fig leaves for coverings. They tried to hide from God when He called out and said, "Where are you?" He was not asking them for their physical location. He was saying, "Where are you in your relationship with Me?"

How long and how many times had satan tried to deceive Eve? We don't know, but I'm sure just like he does with us, he will keep trying to wear us down until one day he finds us weak and we give in to his temptation.

The good news, God is a God of second chances and more if we need it. The testimonies in the Bible give us hope and encouragement for our daily life.

We see Eve's redemption in Genesis 4:25-26: And Adam knew his wife again, and she bore a son and named him Seth, "For God has appointed another seed for me instead of Abel, whom Cain killed." And as for Seth, to him also a son was born; and he named him Enosh. *Then men began to call on the name of the LORD."*

I love those words: "God has appointed another seed for me." Seth means to establish. The ancestry of Jesus Christ can be traced to the line of Seth! Before Eve had a problem, God had an answer.

This is why I love the testimonies in the Bible; they are tools that equip us to walk in our purpose and carry a prophetic anointing, releasing creative power to bring our dreams and visions to reality. Meditating on the testimonies train our mind to think from the realm of faith. When we forget the works of God, we lose sight of His supernatural ability to rescue us from our challenges of life. Don't give up, no matter what has happened in your life or what you have done. Redemption is near; it is in your mouth!

The Bible, the Word of God, is the owner's manual to life. It was written by the Original Designer and shares how life was intended to function. It instructs us how to maintain, operate and troubleshoot life.

The Bible was never intended to be just an informational book, but a transformational living Word to be desired and highly valued in our life. God's Word will never affect your life until you open your heart and allow the Holy Spirit to open the eyes of your understanding, imparting revelation knowledge of the mysteries of the Kingdom of Heaven.

Psalm 119:89 says, "Forever, O LORD, Your word is settled in heaven." This Scripture talks about the place of God's Word in heaven.

Psalm 119:97 says, "Oh, how I love Your law! It is my meditation all the day." This Scripture places God's Word in David's heart. This is the objective for every believer to fill their heart with God's Word from the heavenly realm.

God's Word never affects our life until it becomes personal. It is not a Word for someone else; it is for you!

> GOD'S WORD NEVER AFFECTS OUR LIFE UNTIL IT BECOMES PERSONAL

We read in Acts 13:22, "I have found David the son of Jesse, a man after My own heart, who will do all My will." This is the testimony I desire. What was David's secret?

David allowed God's Word to govern his actions and help make daily decisions to lead him through the trials of life. David was not a perfect man and the Bible clearly shares his downfalls, but as we read the Psalms, we can see David learned to repent and strengthen himself in the Lord, and no matter what the situation he filled his heart with praise to the Lord!

The Word is life to those who find it and health to their body. It's all about the condition of your heart that allows the Word to become personal to you. A bitter, hardened heart does not hear the voice of God and therefore cannot follow Him.

Values are important in life; they set the standard for your life. There is only one source of power that can stand against the pressure of society—the power of the Holy Spirit. Your character developed from the Word of God will sustain you and protect you from the pitfalls in life.

> **VALUES ARE IMPORTANT IN LIFE; THEY SET THE STANDARD FOR YOUR LIFE**

James 1:21 NLT tells us, "So get rid of all the filth and evil in your lives, and humbly accept the word God has planted in your hearts, for it has the power to save your souls." God's Word produces faith to receive what God has provided for you. And we know that without faith it is impossible to please God. (Hebrews 11:6)

Do you see the Bible as a take it or leave it book? Or do you value God's Word as the final authority in your life?

Are you willing to make a personal commitment to pursue and experience the life-giving Word of God?

"Your word is a lamp to my feet
And a light to my path."
PSALM 119:105

POINTS TO PONDER

Meditate on 2 Timothy 3:16-17

- A major concern regarding today's church is that we have lost our love for God's Word.
- We must determine values in our life and set boundaries.
- The testimonies in the Bible give us hope and encouragement for our daily life.
- The Bible, the Word of God, is the owner's manual to life.
- The Bible was never intended to be just an informational book, but a transformational living Word to be desired and highly valued in our lives.
- God's Word never affects our life until it becomes personal. It is not a Word for someone else; it is for you!
- It is all about the condition of your heart that allows the Word to become personal to you.

CHAPTER 3

THE *Power* OF THE *Word* OF *God*

"For the word of God is alive and powerful. It is sharper than the sharpest two-edged sword, cutting between soul and spirit, between joint and marrow. It exposes our innermost thoughts and desires."
HEBREWS 4:12 NLT

The Bible is not simply words about God; it is the Word of God. The Bible is the voice of God in print.

"God has spoken once, twice I have heard this: that power belongs to God" (Psalms 62:11). The power of God is in His Word! People long for the power of God working in their lives and delivering them from the corruption of the world, yet they forget that Jesus has said, "The seed is the word of God" (Luke 8:11).

In 1 Peter 1:23 we read, "Having been born again, not of corruptible seed but incorruptible, through the word of God which lives and abides forever." The process is simply this: The human heart is the soil; you and I are sowers and the Word of God is the seed dropped into the soil of our heart. New life is imparted, and our spirit becomes a "new creation" in Christ Jesus!

Now, we are to become partakers of the divine nature of God. How do we do that? Again, through God's Word. Second Peter 1:4 says, "By which have been given to us exceedingly great and precious promises, that through these you may be partakers of the divine nature, having escaped the corruption *that is* in the world through lust." The Word of God is the seed planted, and the Holy Spirit brings revelation to our mind so that we can understand the mysteries of the Kingdom of God. (Matthew 13:11).

God's Word imparts wisdom and builds character in those who seek Him. "The entrance of Your words gives light; it gives understanding to the simple" (Psalm 119:130). As a new Christian, we must grow in the grace and knowledge of the Lord. His Word must be revealed to us by the Holy Spirit, and that Word gives us faith and confidence in our daily life.

Many people are longing and seeking for peace in this world, but only God's Word planted in our heart can keep us in perfect peace. Psalm 85:8 NLT tells us, "I listen carefully to what God the LORD is saying, for he speaks peace to his faithful people. But let them not return to their foolish ways."

Jesus speaks some specific words to His disciples in John 14, 15 and 16 as He is preparing them for His departure. Read these chapters and meditate on them. I believe they will bring hope and comfort to you.

John 14:25-27 says, "These things I have spoken to you while being present with you. But the Helper, the Holy Spirit, whom the Father will send in My name, He will teach you all things, and bring to your remembrance all things that I said to you. Peace I leave with you, My peace I give to you; not as the world gives do I give to you. Let not your heart be troubled, neither let it be afraid."

John 15:11 says, "These things I have spoken to you, that My joy may remain in you, and *that* your joy may be full."

John 16:1 states, "These things I have spoken to you, that you should not be made to stumble."

John 16:33 says, "These things I have spoken to you, that in Me you may have peace. In the world you will have tribulation; but be of good cheer, I have overcome the world."

There is one passage in the Bible which, if we feed upon it daily until it becomes life to us, will banish all anxiety forever. Romans 8:28 says, "And we know that all things work together for good to those who love God, to those who are the called according to *His* purpose." All things include all things! If we truly believe this passage, whatever comes will not disturb us or rob our peace. We will be fully persuaded that what God has promised He is able to perform!

Yes, God's Word is alive and powerful! As a born-again child of God, we live in a war zone in this world. First Peter 5:8 tells us, "Be sober, be vigilant; because your adversary the devil walks about like a roaring lion, seeking whom he may devour." If we neglect to feed on the Word of God, we leave an open door for the enemy to come in and tempt us. Jesus met and overcame the temptation of the adversary by the Word of God. He replied, "It is written" (Matthew 4:4, 7, 10).

We are in a battle and we are told to fight the good fight of faith in 1 Timothy 6:12. Faith only comes from the Word of God, and without faith it is impossible to please Him.

Reading and meditating on God's Word is spiritual warfare! Every time you open the Word of God you are preparing for battle. You are sharpening your sword to stop the fiery darts of the enemy!

> READING AND MEDITATING ON GOD'S WORD IS SPIRITUAL WARFARE!

Jesus said the Word of God was like a seed. The Word has the power to grow or cause growth to happen. The Word planted in an obedient heart can change hardened hearts to life-giving vessels generation after generation. Christianity has survived because of the reproductive power contained in the Word. People die and buildings fall apart, but His Word produces the same thing every century—Christians who desire to establish His Church and bring heaven to earth!

Yes, we must value the Word of God because it is life to those who find it. "My son, pay attention to what I say; turn your ear to my words. Do not let them out of your sight, keep them within your heart; for they are life to those who find them and health to one's whole body. Above all else, guard your heart, for everything you do flows from it" (Proverbs 4:20-23 NIV).

Eve made a choice with her voice! She chose to believe a lie of the enemy and empowered the liar. Romans 6:16 NLT tells us, "Don't you realize that you become the slave of whatever you choose to obey? You can be a slave to sin, which leads to death, or you can choose to obey God, which leads to righteous living."

> *"In the beginning was the Word, and the Word was with God, and the Word was God."*
> JOHN 1:1

POINTS TO PONDER

Meditate on Proverbs 4:20-23.

- The Bible is not simply words about God; it is the Word of God. The Bible is the voice of God in print.
- God's Word imparts wisdom and builds character in those who seek Him.
- All things include all things! Romans 8:28 - If we honestly believe this passage, whatever comes will not disturb us or rob our peace.
- Every time you open the Word of God you are preparing for battle. You are sharpening your sword to stop the fiery darts of the enemy!
- Eve made a choice with her voice!
- Reading and meditating the Word of God is spiritual warfare.

CHAPTER 4

THE *Power* OF YOUR *Words*

*"Death and life are in the power of the tongue,
and those who love it will eat its fruit."*
PROVERBS 18:21

In the beginning where it all started, words were the vehicle God used in the spiritual realm to make something happen in the natural realm. When God wanted something physical to happen, He spoke.

Over and over in Genesis 1 we see the words, "And God said...." God simply speaks as He does the amazing work of creating the universe!

Genesis 1:26-27 states: "Then God said, 'Let Us make man in Our image, according to Our likeness; let them have dominion over the fish of the sea, over the birds of the air, and over the cattle, over all the earth and over every creeping thing that creeps on the earth.' So God created man in His *own* image; in the image of God He created him; male and female He created them."

We read in Genesis 2:7, "And the LORD God formed man *of* the dust of the ground, and breathed into his nostrils the breath of life; and man became a living being." We are more than just the dust of the earth. God has breathed spirit into us!

We are the only species on earth that can communicate with our hearts. We have feelings, dreams, hopes and plans. There is something creative and powerful with the words that we speak. This is very clear as we study and read the Word of God.

We can see this principle in Eve's life. With the words of her mouth she lost her authority in the Garden and gave satan permission to steal her joy and peace. She lost her position in the Garden of Eden. Her physical body was still in the Garden, but she lost her position in the spiritual realm and her relationship with God.

A key for us to remember is, God bridges the gap to us through words and we connect to Him the same way. There is not a better Scripture that shows us the heart–mouth connection than Romans 10:8-13.

"But what does it say? 'The word is near you, in your mouth and in your heart' (that is, the word of faith which we preach): that if you confess with your mouth the Lord Jesus and believe in your heart that God has raised Him from the dead, you will be saved. For with the heart one believes unto righteousness, and with the mouth confession is made unto salvation. For the Scripture says, 'Whoever believes on Him will not be put to shame.' For there is no distinction between Jew and Greek, for the same Lord over all is rich to all who call upon Him. For 'whoever calls on the name of the LORD shall be saved.'"

This is powerful! By the words of your mouth, speaking what you believe in your heart, you are born again! You are now a child of God! John 1:12 says, "But as many as received Him, to them He gave the right to become children of God, to those who believe in His name." You were translated from the dominion of darkness into the Kingdom of Light by the words of your mouth.

We must also remember that when the serpent approached Eve in the Garden to deceive her, he also used words. He said to Eve, "Has God indeed said…?" (Genesis 3:1). Just as God uses words, satan uses words to deceive and twist God's Word. He always uses a little bit of truth and that is why we must know the Word of God and be open to the Holy Spirit to know the truth that only God speaks to us. Words that cause us to doubt God's Word and move us from an attitude of gratitude to grumbling and from praise to self-pity and discourage us from prayer is a plot of the enemy.

We were created in God's image and likeness. When we are born again and become a new creation in Christ Jesus our spirit is alive, and it is given to us to know the mysteries of the Kingdom of God. Matthew 13:11 tells us, "Because it has been given to you to know the mysteries of the kingdom of heaven, but to them it has not been given."

Hebrews 11:3 says, "By faith we understand that the worlds were framed by the word of God, so that the things which are seen were not made of things which are visible." Meditating this Scripture one day, the Lord whispered to my heart, "Frame your world with My Word." I immediately started writing Scriptures out and placing them around my house. This is a wonderful way to help keep your mind focused on who you are and what God has done for you!

Your Creator has given you the power to agree with Him and speak His Word, thereby creating faith to receive His promises. Jesus tells us in John 6:63, "It is the Spirit who gives life; the flesh profits nothing. The words that I speak to you are spirit, and *they are life.*"

Always keep in your mind that you are a "new creation in Christ Jesus," and we are speaking about how you live your new creation life as you walk the runway of life. One phrase I purpose to think on and speak continually is, "I am a child of God! I am no longer a slave to fear!"

I'm not saying we have the power to just speak anything we want or create a universe like God. I am saying we are made in His image and God told us in Isaiah 57:19, "I create the fruit of the lips...." As we meditate the Word of God and grow in faith, we come into agreement with what God's Word says and it becomes life to us. Out of the abundance of the heart the mouth speaks. This is the very foundation of

> **THE KEY ISSUE HERE IS BELIEVING IN OUR HEART**

our faith. We believe in our heart and speak with our mouth. The key issue here is believing in our heart. I said the sinner's prayer several times and was never saved because I did not believe in my heart and they were empty words.

Second Corinthians 4:13 says, "And since we have the same spirit of faith, according to what is written, 'I believed and therefore I spoke,' we also believe and therefore speak." The heart-mouth sin is the sin that can also break our fellowship with God, and it is also the tool to reconnect us with God. First John 1:9 says, "If we confess (words) our sins, He is faithful and just to forgive us *our* sins and to cleanse us from all unrighteousness."

Sometimes we just mess up! If you do, I have good news for you, as He promised He has also made a way of escape. All you must do is swallow your pride and go humbly to your Father and ask for forgiveness.

A good Scripture to frame your world with is Psalm 19:14, "Let the words of my mouth and the meditation of my heart be acceptable in Your sight, O LORD, my strength and my Redeemer."

Isaiah 54:17 says, "No weapon formed against you shall prosper, and every tongue *which* rises against you in judgment you shall condemn. This *is* the heritage of the servants of the LORD, and their righteousness *is* from Me, says the LORD." How do you condemn every tongue that lies about you or that betrays you? First, you forgive them, just as Christ forgave you. Then you speak what God says about you! YOUR heritage, your birthright, is to speak the Word of God! We need to follow Jesus' example: "It is written" (Luke 4:10).

Proverbs 4:20-23 NIV is what I call a foundational Scripture, "My son, pay attention to what I say; turn your ear to my words. Do not let them out of your sight, keep them within your heart; for they are life to those who find them and health to one's whole body. Above all else, guard your heart, for everything you do flows from it."

We must build a strong foundation to help us in our daily life. A foundation is a load-bearing part of a building. If the foundation is unstable, it can be blown away by every wind of doctrine. A foundation in not seen, but most cracks in a home come from foundation issues. A problem which we do not see is causing a problem that we do see. Many people today are just interested in filling up cracks and painting over them.

Our character is the foundation built by the Word of God that will keep us through the trials and temptations of life. Character will sustain us through our journey as we cultivate the garden of our hearts.

I am sure that many of you reading this have at one time heard talk about "the name it, claim it gospel." I agree that there has been a lot of abuse and just plain greediness regarding this principle, just as there has been about the gifts of the Spirit and healing today. It is only the truth that can set us free and open the eyes of our understanding! Proverbs 4:22 NIV says, "For they are life to those who find them and health to one's whole body." We have a lot of lazy Christians who want everything handed to them.

I'm a person who doesn't like to read directions. I always say to my husband, "Read the directions and tell me what to do." Well, it doesn't work that way with the gospel. It is based on a personal relationship with God. Your success depends on renewing your mind daily by meditating on the Word of God.

At the new birth, our spirits receive the life of God. Our next need is that our minds be renewed. Before we came into the family of God, we walked as a natural man. Satan ruled our minds because we were ignorant. Romans 12:2 NLT says, "Don't copy the behavior and customs of this world, but let God transform you into a new person by changing the way you think. Then you will learn to know God's will for you, which is good and pleasing and perfect." We must renew our minds so that we will know our privileges and responsibilities as children of God.

The new birth is instantaneous, but the renewing of our mind is a gradual process determined by our study and meditation on the Word of God. So don't allow what others think about the gospel to rule you and thereby miss out on the blessings of the Lord.

Study the book of Proverbs. The key word in Proverbs is wisdom, the ability to live life skillfully. Living a godly life in an ungodly world is no simple assignment. Proverbs gives God's detailed instructions for you to deal successfully with the practical affairs of everyday life. It shares common sense and divine perspective necessary to handle life's issues. One of the major topics is the heart-mouth issues of life.

Proverbs 18:20-21 says, "A man's stomach shall be satisfied *from* the fruit of his mouth; from the produce of his lips he shall be filled.

Death and life are in the power of the tongue, and those who love it will eat its fruit." Are you satisfied with your life? Are you filled with the produce of your lips? Is your life full of joy, or do you dread getting out of bed?

Proverbs 15:4 says, "A wholesome tongue is a tree of life, but perverseness in it breaks the spirit." Only words can break a spirit! It is very hard to recover from a wounded spirit.

Proverbs 6:2 says, "You are snared by the words of your mouth; you are taken by the words of your mouth." Stop blaming others for your life situation. Take responsibility for your thoughts and actions. Nobody has a perfect family life! Nobody forced you to make a decision. Get over it. God is for you. He is not against you, and He said nothing can separate you from His love. Read the Word. You are created in God's image. He knew you in your mother's womb!

> TAKE RESPONSIBILITY FOR YOUR THOUGHTS AND ACTIONS

Next to Proverbs, the book of James gives us some practical steps to walk in true faith in our everyday life. James brings us face to face with the fact that, "But no man can tame the tongue. *It is* an unruly evil, full of deadly poison. With it we bless our God and Father, and with it we curse men, who have been made in the similitude of God. Out of the same mouth proceed blessing and cursing. My brethren, these things ought not to be so" (James 3:8-10).

Have you submitted your tongue to God? That is a good place to start. Please read and meditate on the words of James. It will change your life.

Lastly, let's look at Matthew 12:33-37, "Either make the tree good and its fruit good, or else make the tree bad and its fruit bad; for a tree is known by *its* fruit. Brood of vipers! How can you, being evil, speak good things? For out of the abundance of the heart the mouth speaks. A good man out of the good treasure of his heart brings forth good things, and an evil man out of the evil treasure brings forth evil things. But I say to you that for every idle word men may speak, they will give account of it in the day of judgment. For by your words you will be justified, and by your words you will be condemned."

A tree is known by its fruit! The words that come out of our mouths are a direct indicator of what is in our heart. I personally wish Jesus hadn't mentioned idle words. We have all said some dumb things! Remember, we are in a process called life; we have not arrived yet. By the grace of God when we confess our sins, He is faithful and just to cleanse us and remember them no more! This includes sins of the mouth.

IT IS TIME WE RAISE THE STANDARD OF OUR LIFE

It is time we raise the standard of our life. Stop speaking death over your life, your family, your health and finances. Speak words that agree with God's Word.

As we have seen in the Scriptures, you are either agreeing with God's Word which gives life or agreeing with satan's words which have one purpose and that is to steal, kill and destroy. *The choice is yours.*

When Adam and Eve sinned, it was not a shock to God. He was well aware of the risk in giving them a free will. His desire was for sons and daughters who would love Him and that requires a choice. God's purpose for mankind has not changed. His desire is still to establish His Kingdom on earth by co-laboring with His children. Through the "new birth" we are to be fruitful and multiply and fill the earth. His dominion is extended throughout the world through His covenant relationship with those He made in His image and who worship Him by choice.

Remember, your words carry the power of life and death. What a responsibility and what a privilege!

> *"The preparations of the heart belong to man, but the answer of the tongue is from the LORD."*
> PROVERBS 16:1

POINTS TO PONDER

Read and meditate the Book of Proverbs.

- We are the only species on earth who can communicate with our hearts.
- By the words of your mouth and speaking what you believe in your heart, you are born again!
- Your Creator has given you the power to agree with Him and speak His Word, thereby creating His life with your words.
- We must build a strong foundation to help us in our daily life.
- The new birth is instantaneous, but the renewing of our mind is a gradual process determined by our study and meditation on the Word of God.
- It is time we raise the standard of our life. Stop speaking death over your life, your family, your health and finances. Speak words that agree with God's Word.
- It is not a "word" problem; it is a "heart" problem!

CHAPTER 5

EMBRACING
God's Word

*"But I fear, lest somehow, as the serpent deceived
Eve by his craftiness, so your minds may be
corrupted from the simplicity that is in Christ."*
2 CORINTHIANS 11:3

Paul understood the battleground is in your mind. This is the battlefield as we walk the runway of life where decisions are made that determine our course of life.

Second Corinthians 10:3-5 tells us, "For though we walk in the flesh, we do not war according to the flesh. For the weapons of our warfare are not carnal but mighty in God for pulling down strongholds, casting down arguments and every high thing that exalts itself against the knowledge of God, bringing every thought into captivity to the obedience of Christ."

Your mind, which is part of your soul, is the battlefield of your spiritual life living in this natural world. What you choose to listen to and what you choose to think on will set the course of your life. Many thoughts enter your mind, but you do not have to think on every thought that enters your mind. God has given you the power of choice and that is where it all begins. Paul is warning us that we must guard what enters our mind because this is what brought the downfall of Eve. She took thought of what the serpent said and spoke it from her mouth. As a result, her mind was corrupted, and confusion set in.

One thought can change your life for good or destruction. *The most important thing we can learn from Eve is the power of choice.* Once you make a choice, you become a servant to that choice. Circumstances in your life do not determine your level of life. Today we see a "victim mentality." No one wants to take responsibility for the choices they make. Your life is composed of choices. When you claim victim status, you are not accepting responsibility for your own choices. Choices have consequences.

> THE MOST IMPORTANT THING WE CAN LEARN FROM EVE IS THE POWER OF CHOICE

Life is composed of our choices and constructed by our words. If you do not take the responsibility to make choices, you are allowing others to make choices for you and create your world. No one knows your mind and heart; that is between you and God. You can complain all you want, but if you are not willing to make choices in your life, others will control your life. Regardless of the circumstances of your life, you still have the power of choice! The choices you make today will determine your tomorrow. Choices determine conduct and character. The right choice will sustain the gifts that God has imparted to you.

Once you make a choice to change and build a new life, you have to change your words. Our words build our lives, and every word has creative power. We release our future and set the world around us in motion by the creative power of our words. Use your words wisely and you will prosper. Your choices and your words are two of your best tools you have for building life. (We covered this in Chapter 4 of this book.)

Your greatest choice in life is asking God to forgive you of your sins and receiving Jesus as your Lord and Savior. Second, you must forgive yourself. Your life before the cross is over, buried. Now you must release forgiveness towards those who hurt you, betrayed you, lied to you and caused pain and grief in your life.

Only by the power of the Holy Spirit can you forgive others that have used and abused you. Forgiving others will release you from the bondage of their words. This is the simplicity of the gospel to forgive as God forgave you, but it is probably one of the hardest things we have to do.

> ONLY BY THE POWER OF THE HOLY SPIRIT CAN YOU FORGIVE OTHERS THAT HAVE USED AND ABUSED YOU

I believe one of the biggest problems in the Church today is that most Christians understand they have been forgiven, but do not fully understand the purpose of forgiveness or the power of forgiveness. If we do not understand what we have been given by forgiveness of our sins, we will not be able to pursue and experience the benefits given to the child of God.

Second Corinthian 5:17 NLT says, "This means that anyone who belongs to Christ has become a new person. The old life is gone; a new life has begun!" Forgiveness cleanses us from all unrighteousness, and we are a total new creation in Christ Jesus. The only place your past lives is in your mind, and that is why your mind must be renewed by the Word of God. Galatians 6:16 NLT tells us, "May God's peace and mercy be upon all who live by this principle; they are the new people of God." Only the Holy Spirit can reveal to us the purpose of forgiveness and our rights and privileges as a "new creation" in Christ Jesus.

You were created in His image as a new creation instantly, but you are being formed into His likeness as you do everyday life and learn from the trials and temptations in the world. It is a lifetime pursuit.

God is making His people to be "fruitful and multiply" through the new birth by the power of the Holy Spirit. As John 1:12-13 puts it, "But as many as received Him, to them He gave the right to become children of God, to those who believe in His name: who were born, not of blood, nor of the will of the flesh, nor of the will of man, but of God."

Our right to become children of God gives us access to a relationship as Jesus has with the Father. Thankfully, Jesus modeled this for us as He walked on earth as a man. Luke 2:52 shares with us, "And Jesus increased in wisdom and stature, and in favor with God and men." Hebrews 5:8 says, "Though He was a Son, *yet* He learned obedience by the things which He suffered." Study the gospels to learn how Jesus did life on earth.

Adam and Eve forfeited the authority given to them to the serpent in the Garden. God prepared the world for deliverance through Jesus and through faithful men and women who surrender their will to Him.

God has included the testimonies of faithful men and women in the Bible so we can learn from their examples and have hope in this world. First Corinthians 10:11 NLT tells us, "These things happened to them as examples for us. They were written down to warn us who live at the end of the age." The Psalmist said, "Your testimonies I have taken as a heritage forever, for they are the rejoicing of my heart. (Psalm 119:111) The testimonies recorded in the Word of God are my eternal possession and contain the resources that I need to be transformed into the likeness of Christ, demonstrating and releasing God's power in the earth today!

I am encouraged when I study the life of Jochebed. Most Christians do not even know who she is. She is referred to as "the mother of Moses" in Scriptures. You only know her name if you read the begets. She is mentioned by name twice in the Bible, in Exodus 6:20 and in Numbers 26:59. The testimony of her life tells us it is not so much who you are, but what you do with your life and how you meet life's crises and responsibilities that matter.

Everyone knows Moses, but his mother set the stage for him to lead the children of Israel out of bondage. Read her testimony in Exodus 2 and Hebrews 11:23. What about Esther, an orphan who saved her nation from disaster? Study David, one young man who learned in the fields tending sheep. Unknown by man, even his own family did not include him when Samuel came looking for the next king. One thing these testimonies show me is, it does not take an army, God only needs one faithful person with a heart to know Him and walk in obedience to bring deliverance!

Study the men and women in the Bible so you can learn. All through the Psalms God speaks of declaring the works of God. In Psalm 111:2 we read, "The works of the LORD *are* great, studied by all who have pleasure in them." In what do you have pleasure?

Every testimony is an unveiling of God's nature and an invitation to know and experience the same power in our life. Understanding the power of the testimony in our life as a child of God positions us to experience God in what He desires to do through us in the present.

Either we allow the revelation of who He is to transform the way we think and perceive reality from God's perspective, or we resist the truth and become hard-hearted.

> AS A NEW CREATION IN CHRIST, THERE IS NO NEUTRAL TERRITORY IN OUR WORLD

As a new creation in Christ, there is no neutral territory in our world. Our heart (spirit) is the gate to the spiritual realm and our thoughts become words that open the gate. Whatever fills our heart and mind brings us to a place of agreement. Either we will be filled with joy and peace during our struggles of life, or fear and anxiety will take over our lives.

As we study the testimony of Eve, we can see and understand that our power of choice creates the life we are living today. The good news is that we also see the testimony of her redemption in Genesis 4:25, "For God has appointed another seed for me…." Eve's testimony gives me hope. No matter what my past is, I have a future that God has ordained for me! As I grow in my spiritual life and learn to "hear" His voice, He leads me into my purpose for life.

The fall of man in the Garden failed to diminish God's plan in having an earth filled with people who live in relationship with Him, people He walks with as He did with Adam and Eve in the Garden.

God's desire is still to establish His Kingdom on the earth by co-laboring with His children, those He created in His image, who worship Him by choice. *This is the purpose of our forgiveness, that we can be made whole again and receive our inheritance in Christ Jesus.*

As we learn to receive and walk in our inheritance in Christ Jesus, we must also understand the power of forgiveness in our lives. As we receive forgiveness, we must give forgiveness. This is a key to living in the Kingdom of God and enjoying our benefits of peace and joy in the Holy Spirit. Ephesians 4:32 says, "And be kind to one another, tenderhearted, forgiving one another, even as God in Christ forgave you."

Matthew 6:15 makes it noticeably clear, "But if you do not forgive men their trespasses, neither will your Father forgive your trespasses."

Second Corinthians 2:10-11 says, "Now whom you forgive anything, I also *forgive*. For if indeed I have forgiven anything, I have forgiven that one for your sakes in the presence of Christ, lest Satan should take advantage of us; for we are not ignorant of his devices." Unforgiveness is an open door for the enemy. Remember, the devil walks about like a roaring lion, seeking an open door. (See 1 Peter 5:8.)

John 20:21-23 gives us more insight, So Jesus said to them again, "Peace to you! As the Father has sent Me, I also send you." And when He had said this, He breathed on *them*, and said to them, "Receive the Holy Spirit. If you forgive the sins of any, they are forgiven them; if you retain the sins of any, they are retained."

These Scriptures make it clear that our new creation life on earth starts with receiving forgiveness and as we walk in our new life on earth, we must freely give forgiveness. I personally believe from the Word of God and personal experience, forgiving those who have wronged you can only be done as we submit to the Holy Spirit asking Him to help us. Jesus breathed on them, and said, "Receive the Holy Spirit" and then told them to forgive.

Forgetting is also part of forgiving. When you continually dwell on the past hurts and heartache in your mind, your thoughts hold you in bondage. First John 1:9 says, "If we confess our sins, He is faithful and just to forgive us *our* sins and to cleanse us from all unrighteousness." There are two parts to forgiveness: forgive and cleanse. Forgiveness is instant, but cleansing takes time. The cleansing takes place by the washing of the water of the Word. If you see or have a thought about the person who hurt you and the pain of that hurt hits you and the devil says you did not forgive them, remember, he is a liar. You are in the cleansing phase and that takes time.

Forgiveness is a choice. As a child of God, your first thought when you are hurt and feel the pain of rejection should be to forgive! God told us in Mark 11:25-26, "And whenever you stand praying, if you have anything against anyone, forgive him, that your Father in heaven may also forgive you your trespasses. But if you do not forgive, neither will your Father in heaven forgive your trespasses." *When you stand praying!* That is now, not down the road after you have waddled in self-pity and walked around the same old mountain one more time.

> FORGIVENESS IS A CHOICE, AND AS A CHILD OF GOD, IT SHOULD BE YOUR FIRST THOUGHT WHEN YOU ARE HURT

As I said, forgiveness is a choice. I made that choice many years ago when I was fighting a battle in my life. My daughter's hair caught on fire. As I was walking down the hall, she ran out of her bedroom with flames shooting from her hair! I screamed, JESUS! As I reached up to try to beat the flames out, the instant my hands touched her hair, the flames went out! She had severe burns to her scalp and the doctor said her hair follicles had been destroyed and the hair would not grow back, I said, "we know the God that created hair follicles"!

The next week I was in the grocery store when a woman from our church approached me saying, "Joyce, do you know what so and so said about you?" This woman was a "thorn" in my life at that time.

I felt anger rise up within me, but before I could speak, I had a flash back of my daughter running with flames shooting from her hair, and the Lord whispered to me, "Joyce, it's not worth it."

From that moment, I made a choice to forgive and I have never wrestled with forgiveness in my life since. I am saying to you today you will have many opportunities to walk in unforgiveness, it is not worth it! I choose to guard my heart and receive the blessings of the Lord.

The good news is my daughter was totally and miraculously healed from the injury and the shock! And she has beautiful hair today and much to the amazement of the doctor, my hands never showed any signs of touching the flames. God is faithful!

Many people tell me, "I'm trying to forgive." You do not try; you do it! You make a choice to forgive for your well-being, not for the person who hurt you. It is okay to cry! Let those tears wash away the hurt. Guard your friendships. You probably need to stop some relationships from your past, especially those that try to pull you down to their level. Jesus is NOW your best Friend!

God has given us a way of escape through forgiving those who lie about you, betray you and abuse you. Remember, if you do not forgive, you retain the sin. I have seen this in alcoholics, drug users and abusers. Many were brought up in homes where these addictions ruled. When we do not forgive the hurt and pain of this lifestyle, we will retain the sin and not understand why we continue doing what we hated in our life.

Many people call this generational curse. I believe the only way to break a generational curse is to forgive.

Paul says in Philippians 3:13 NLT, "No, dear brothers and sisters, I have not achieved it, but I focus on this one thing: *Forgetting the past and looking forward to what lies ahead.*"

As I was meditating that Scripture one day, I was frustrated and I said, "God, how do I forget? You know the enemy keeps reminding me of everything I have ever done wrong."

He immediately answered me and said, "*You remember.*" I was not expecting that. Remember? As I pondered on this, He said, "When you remember, you are choosing your thoughts!" *Wow, what a revelation!* I chose to walk in that revelation, choosing the thoughts that I think on.

> WHEN YOU REMEMBER, YOU ARE CHOOSING YOUR THOUGHTS!

If you are not choosing your thoughts, satan will use your mind as his playground! Again, it is a personal choice. Remembering brings us to an attitude of gratitude and thanksgiving. "Be thankful in all circumstances, for this is God's will for you who belong to Christ Jesus" (1Thessalonians 5:18 NLT). Notice, this is the will of God! Many ask me, "How do I know the will of God?" I always respond, "You read and meditate on God's Word." *That is the simplicity of the gospel of Jesus Christ.*

Meditating on the testimonies and remembering those who have walked before us give us a foundation on which to build our new creation life. When we remember what God has done and meditate on it, it becomes life to us. We take the "seed" of the Word from a testimony into our heart and it becomes life to us, and another miracle comes forth in our life!

I love John 14:26, "But the Helper, the Holy Spirit, whom the Father will send in My name, He will teach you all things, and bring to your remembrance all things that I said to you." The Holy Spirit brings to your remembrance what you have put into your heart. So many times, in my life the Holy Spirit breathed in my life just the right Scripture at just the right time to bring deliverance in a situation in my life. The Seed of the Word had been hidden in my heart, and the Holy Spirit pulled it out and brought it to my remembrance in my time of need.

I am so thankful that I do not have to memorize the whole Bible. I'm not saying memorizing is not good. I find that when I meditate on the Word and the Holy Spirit brings revelation and insight, it is implanted in my heart and no one can steal that Word from me.

This is what I call "seedtime and harvest!" Genesis 8:22 says, "While the earth remains, seedtime and harvest, cold and heat, winter and summer, and day and night shall not cease." Life is all about the seed sown in your heart.

We must take heed of what Proverbs 4:23 NIV tells us: "Above all else, guard your heart, for everything you do flows from it." Our heart is the Garden through which the spirit realm connects with the natural realm, and our thoughts and words open the gate to our heart. What we choose to focus on—either the reality of God's Kingdom based on truth, or the destruction reality of the enemy's kingdom, established on lies—gives permission for that reality to flow from our heart.

I have found in my personal life, what I value I purpose to give my time to. Time is your greatest asset. We all have the same amount of time; 60 seconds in a minute and eternity is in it. Investing a small amount of time over time in things that matter most brings increase in your life.

As I said, time is your greatest asset and choice is your only freedom in life. Eve's downfall in the Garden, she did not value God's Word and chose to listen to the twisted, deceiving word of the enemy. In doing this she empowered the liar to ruin her life in the Garden. But the good news is, no matter how low you sink, there is always redemption.

Yes, we have much to learn from this first lady of the Garden. Open your heart to Eve and ask the Holy Spirit to teach you from this woman's testimony.

> *"And they have defeated him by the blood of the Lamb and by their testimony. And they did not love their lives so much that they were afraid to die."*
> REVELATION 12:11 NLT

POINTS TO PONDER

Meditate on 2 Corinthians 11:3

- Paul understood the battleground is in your mind.
- God has given you the power of choice and that is where it all begins.
- Life is composed of our choices and constructed by our words.
- Choices determine conduct and character.
- Once you make a choice, you become a servant to that choice.
- As we study the testimony of Eve, we can see and understand that our power of choice creates the life we are living today.
- Every testimony is an unveiling of God's nature and an invitation to know and experience the same power in our life.
- God has given us a way of escape through forgiving those who lie about us and betray us.
- Forgiveness is a choice.
- Meditating on the testimonies and remembering those who have walked before us give us a foundation on which to build our new creation life.

CHAPTER 6

Plant YOUR OWN *Garden*

"The seed is the word of God."
LUKE 8:11

There are many Christians frustrated, full of anxiety and discouraged. As I talk with them, it becomes evident they do not understand the principle of seedtime and harvest. They are waiting on someone else to plant a seed and bring them flowers. Always looking for "a word" from someone to tell them what to do.

I love the prophetic ministry, but more than that I love hearing the "voice" of God in my spirit. John 10:27 says, "My sheep hear My voice, and I know them, and they follow Me."

I have received many prophetic words in my lifetime, and they always confirm what God spoke to me! They brought comfort and encouragement for me to walk in obedience to what God had whispered in my spirit.

To receive your miracle, you must first plant a seed. The power of God is in the seed of His Word! If you consistently sow the promises of God into your heart, you will reap whatever that Word promises. You were born again because you heard God's promise of salvation that if you believe in your heart and confess with your mouth you would be saved. (See Romans 10:9-10.)

Sowing healing promises into your heart results in a harvest of healing. Sowing provision promises into your heart results in a harvest of provision. Each seed brings forth according to its kind. If you need peace and joy, pull up some weeds and plant some seeds!

In Mark 4:26-29 NLT, Jesus also said, "The Kingdom of God is like a farmer who scatters seed on the ground. Night and day, while he's asleep or awake, the seed sprouts and grows, but he does not understand how it happens. The earth produces the crops on its own. First a leaf blade pushes through, then the heads of wheat are formed, and finally the grain ripens. And as soon as the grain is ready, the farmer comes and harvests it with a sickle, for the harvest time has come."

There is a germination process of the Word of God in your life that takes time and cannot be avoided. You must see the blade before the seed ripens and is ready for harvest. Have you prepared your heart to receive the harvest?

I don't understand how it all works, but I know my responsibility and that is to plant the seed, cultivate the soil of my heart to receive the seed and expect a harvest! As I am waiting for the harvest, I must keep the weeds of unforgiveness, anger, jealousy and the cares of the world from choking the seeds I have sown. One secret I have learned through many trials of life is that patience is the power that pushes the seed forward.

James 1:4 says, "But let patience have its perfect work, that you may be perfect and complete, lacking nothing." I personally have never met another human being who has enjoyed the wait for the harvest! I have walked with God for forty years and purposed in my heart to grow in the grace and knowledge of God. My trust in God's timing has grown. I am not saying I have arrived; I have learned to be content and confident in God's love for me.

> ONE SECRET I HAVE LEARNED THROUGH MANY TRIALS OF LIFE IS THAT PATIENCE IS THE POWER THAT PUSHES THE SEED FORWARD

I meet many Christians who think salvation is all there is and are living a miserable life on this earth. God's Word tells us that He has given us everything we need for life and godliness. (See 2 Peter 1:2-4)

Most Christians have an escape mentally! They want to escape the hard times we face in this world. Jesus also said, "These things I have spoken to you, that in Me you may have peace. In the world you will have tribulation; but be of good cheer, I have overcome the world" (John 16:33).

We cannot always avoid the trials of life, but we can develop daily habits that prepare us, and we can learn to strengthen our self in the Lord. Life in this world is about aligning your life with the heart of God.

Jesus had been teaching the parable of the sower. When He was alone with His disciples, they asked Him about this parable, Then Jesus said to them, "If you can't understand the meaning of this parable, how will you understand all the other parables?" (Mark 4:13 NLT). These words should burn in your heart. Meditate on this parable, asking the Holy Spirit for insight.

Understanding this parable is foundational to understanding all other parables. As a new creation in Christ Jesus, we live at a crossroad, the place between mystery and revelation. Matthew 13:11 tells us, He answered and said to them, "Because it has been given to you to know the mysteries of the kingdom of heaven, but to them it has not been given."

Paul instructs us in Ephesians 1:17-18 to ask " that the God of our Lord Jesus Christ, the Father of glory, may give to you the spirit of wisdom and revelation in the knowledge of Him, the eyes of your understanding being enlightened; that you may know what is the hope of His calling, what are the riches of the glory of His inheritance in the saints."

Until the Holy Spirit opens the eyes of our understanding, the Bible is simply printed words. When the Holy Spirit breathes on the Word of God, it becomes life to you! Without revelation you will dry up! With it you will thrive as you understand the mysteries of the Kingdom of Heaven. You are a child of God! The Word of God reveals your inheritance to you. How do you receive revelation? YOU ask! John 16:24 tells us, "Until now you have asked nothing in My name. Ask, and you will receive, that your joy may be full."

> UNTIL THE HOLY SPIRIT OPENS THE EYES OF OUR UNDERSTANDING, THE BIBLE IS SIMPLY PRINTED WORDS

This parable is about three things: the sower, the seed and the soil. The seed is the Word. You are the sower, the person responsible for sowing the seed in your heart. There are four conditions of the soil represented: the wayside soil, hard, unplowed ground. When seed falls on this ground, the enemy immediately steals it before it can take root. The stony soil has no depth and the seed does not grow. Some seed falls on thorny ground full of worries, the deceitfulness of riches and the cares of the world, choking out the growth of the seed. The good ground always yields fruit in season. The good soil has been plowed by repentance. The thorns of life have been cleared bringing forth the fruit of the Spirit.

We must understand there is nothing wrong with the seed, ever! We are responsible for the condition of our heart. A lack of harvest indicates a lack of sowing or a lack of preparation of the soil of your heart. We can also dig up the seed we planted with bad attitudes and failure to water the ground with praise and thanksgiving for our harvest.

There are many life-changing truths in this parable. I urge you to study this parable and listen again to what Jesus said.

God has done His part; He has given us the Word. The Lord doesn't rain money from heaven, but Deuteronomy 8:18 says that the Lord gives us the power to get wealth. The power is in His promises, His Word. As we plant the promises in our heart, the truth is revealed to our spirit and His Word germinates and His blessings flow adding no sorrow to them!

Galatians 6:7-10 NLT states, "Don't be misled—you cannot mock the justice of God. You will always harvest what you plant. Those who live only to satisfy their own sinful nature will harvest decay and death from that sinful nature. But those who live to please the Spirit will harvest everlasting life from the Spirit. So let's not get tired of doing what is good. At just the right time we will reap a harvest of blessing if we don't give up. Therefore, whenever we have the opportunity, we should do good to everyone—especially to those in the family of faith."

Sowing and reaping is a fundamental principle in God's Kingdom. It works for everyone—all the time—for good or for bad, determined by the seeds that were planted.

The quality of our life today is the result of the seeds we have sown in the past. The Word of God is incorruptible seed, designed to be sown into the heart of man.

Another important part in this process is to protect the environment of your heart. As you grow in God many things change. You no longer enjoy hanging out in the old places with friends who do not understand your new life. After accepting Jesus as Lord of our life, the first New Year's Eve, we met our friends at the "old hangout." I'm trying to put on a good face. My husband finally whispered in my ear, "Are you enjoying this?" "NO." He stood up, took my hand and we said good-bye to the old lifestyle.

This is a process. Let God lead you, and He will bring you into your new lifestyle. We need to attend a church where we regularly sit under the anointing of the preaching of God's Word. Our friendships should be with "like-minded believers" who will support us. Yes, I know you are still in this world, and you will be among others who don't understand how good it is to be in Christ Jesus. You are to be the light! But you build relationships with people who will be with you in both the good and bad times.

As I pondered in my heart about Eve I wondered, "Why did Eve become discontent in a perfect world?" As I wrote in Chapter one when I asked God what happened, He spoke to my heart, "She did not value My Word." Eve was discontent, and the door was opened to the enemy. Discontentment is the breeding ground for deception, and that is the only weapon the enemy has to use.

> DISCONTENTMENT IS THE BREEDING GROUND FOR DECEPTION

I have come to the conclusion that when I get to heaven, I will have a heart-to-heart talk with Eve to get all the details. The Word doesn't tell us every detail, and I have learned to accept that. I trust God that He gave us what we need!

In Philippians 4:11 Paul tells us, "…I have learned in whatever state I am, to be content." We were created in God's image, but we are "being formed" into His likeness as we face the detours and trials of life. The simple truth is, we all need help and God has given us the Holy Spirit, the Spirit of truth, to teach us how to overcome in this world.

Jesus said, "If anyone desires to come after Me, let him deny himself, and take up his cross daily, and follow Me" (Luke 9:23). It is a lifelong daily walk, casting down strongholds and every thought that is against the Word of God.

We must build new thought patterns in our soul to renew our minds. The mind is where doubt and unbelief start, which leads to discontentment. Transformation can be messy; we do some dumb things causing us to mess up, and we do not enjoy the wait.

Your part of the transformation process is abiding! John 15:7 says, "If you abide in Me, and My words abide in you, you will ask what you desire, and it shall be done for you." "If" is the biggest little word in the Bible! Every promise in the Word of God has a condition. Study the conditions and find out if you are meeting the conditions to receive the promises.

Nourish your heart, develop a taste for truth and laugh at the devil! Follow the Good Shepherd as He makes you lie down in green pastures and leads you beside the still waters. This is the place He can restore your soul! You are a child of God, no longer a slave to fear, and you have unlimited resources!

> *"The entrance of Your words gives light;*
> *it gives understanding to the simple."*
> PSALM 119:130

POINTS TO PONDER

Study and meditate on The Parable of the Sower:

Matthew 13:1-23 | Mark 4:1-20 | Luke 8:4-15

- Understanding this parable is foundational to understanding all other parables.
- There is a germination process of the Word of God in your life that takes time and cannot be avoided.
- Until the Holy Spirit opens the eyes of our understanding, the Bible is simply printed words.
- Another important part in this process is to protect the environment of your heart.
- Life is a process. Let God lead you, and He will bring you into your new lifestyle.

CHAPTER 7

You WERE *Created* FOR *More*

*"So God created human beings in his own image.
In the image of God he created them;
male and female he created them."*
GENESIS 1:27 NLT

Eve was the crowning touch of God's creative masterpiece. She was not an afterthought, but God's grand finale. With the creation of woman, what was good now became very good!

When Eve received the breath of life the work of God's creation was finished. She was the only one to be perfectly and personally fashioned as a woman by the Creator, and the only woman whose home was Paradise!

God did not create woman simply because man was lonely, He created woman to complete man, to love him, to work with him, to procreate with him and to live life alongside him. She was created as an equal in the Garden.

So what happened? How did the beautiful creation of God move from a mutual place of honor, created in the image and likeness of God, fall from grace and become oppressed, living in bondage for centuries as a victim of abuse and disgrace?

As we read Genesis 3:1, the plot begins to unfold stating, "Now the serpent…." Satan was not happy about the creation of man. Satan had once been an angel of light and had been cast to the earth with one-third of the angels because of their rebellion against God.

He knew he was doomed, and his plan was to take with him those who God had created in His image. We need to understand the strategy behind satan's temptation. The way in which the first human pair were tempted is **still** part of satan's present-day strategy. Understanding how the enemy works gives you the power to resist his temptations and stops the darts of deception from forming in your mind.

Genesis 3:6 says, "So when the woman saw that the tree was good for food, that it was pleasant to the eyes, and a tree desirable to make one wise, she took of its fruit and ate. She also gave to her husband with her, and he ate." "Good for food," *the lust of the flesh.* "Pleasing to the eye," *the lust of the eye.* "Desirable for gaining wisdom," *the pride of life* (1 John 2:16). Satan has no creative abilities, and he is still using this tactic today to plant thoughts in our minds that appeal to our emotions and influence our power of choice.

The serpent, the woman and the man were all judged, but only the serpent and the ground were cursed. God's judgment on the serpent foreshadowed his demise, and he clearly understood it would come from the seed of a woman's womb. "And I will put enmity between you and the woman, and between your seed and her Seed..." (Genesis 3:15). Satan's target has always been and still is the fruit of woman's womb.

In Exodus 1:22, Pharaoh commanded all sons be cast into a river to die. In Matthew 2:16-18 we read that Herod was furious when he was outwitted by the wise men and ordered all boys two years old and under to be killed. Yes, the enemy is still killing the seed of woman's womb by abortion throughout the world today!

If he cannot kill your physical body, he will work at destroying your mental and emotional health so you cannot enjoy your life in this earth. Understanding the creation, the fall and the redemption of mankind is preparation for the battle we face today.

> IF HE CANNOT KILL YOUR PHYSICAL BODY, HE WILL WORK AT DESTROYING YOUR MENTAL AND EMOTIONAL HEALTH

There is good news! You need to be fully persuaded that God loves turning things around. The tree in the Garden brought death and the curse, the tree of Calvary brought life and blessings. Jesus came to set the captives free and to destroy the works of the devil. (1 John 3:8)

Many years passed between the Garden of Eden and the Garden of Gethsemane. Women were devalued, defiled and degraded.

Jesus came not only to destroy the works of satan, but to also restore fallen humanity, which included women restored to their original position before the fall. He called women out of the shadows of society and placed them center stage!

It was a new day for women. Jesus welcomed women into His group and included them in His daily life to be part of His ministry team!

Women were no longer left to walk behind, but to take their rightful place in this earth along the side of men. Jesus came to set women free and in their rightful place in the Kingdom of Heaven.

He set the record straight when He told Martha that Mary had chosen the good part, which would not be taken away from her! He also said, "But one thing is needed," and that remains true to this day for everyone!

> YOUR ONLY NEED IN THIS WORLD IS GOD'S WORD

Your only need in this world is God's Word. You have many desires and wants, but you need to settle in your heart what your greatest need is, the Word of God! (See Luke 10:38-42.)

The desire of the Father is for men and women to walk together in unity, bringing the Kingdom of Heaven to earth! We learn of Him through His Word, showing us His character and His ways.

Jesus came to earth to show us the way. He was the image of the invisible God. We need to look at the life and ministry of God's Son to show us "how to" live as a new creation in Christ Jesus as we walk the runway of life.

Our vision gets clouded by the cares of this world. It is not easy as a child of God in this earth, and we never had a promise that it would be. But God has sent His Word to heal us and deliver us from all destruction.

Study your "family history." Hear their testimonies from a new perspective. Stop going around the same old mountain of self-pity and a distorted view of man's view of God. Sit by the well with the Samaritan woman expecting insults and rejection, but only finding acceptance and love.

Stand with the woman caught in adultery expecting condemnation and death but finding forgiveness and a chance for a new beginning in her life.

Crawl on your knees with the woman with the issue of blood to touch the hem of His garment. Sometimes you have to get down and dirty, to swallow your pride and receive what you do not deserve. Discover what God really thinks of His creation.

God has made the way of escape through forgiveness. You must receive His forgiveness and then continually forgive others. Forgiveness is the way of escape from all the bondage and poverty in this world.

Today's society puts a heavy burden on both men and women with high expectations. Men feel the pressure to perform; women feel the pressure to conform, but God's desire is that we be transformed and He has provided the tool, The Bible, to prepare us for an extraordinary life in the Kingdom of God. As we enter our place of rest in the eternal, we will be free to walk in our uniqueness as women and men of God and be free of the burdens of the world.

Women have influence. Like Eve, we will mess up, many tears will be shed along the path, but through repentance we have been given a way of escape from the pressure of the world.

You, child of God, were given the power and authority to shape the Garden of your life and with your "faith-filled" words form the shield of faith to stop all the fiery darts of the enemy!

> *"**You see**, every child of God overcomes the world, for our faith is the victorious power that triumphs over the world."*
> 1 JOHN 5:4 TPT

POINTS TO PONDER

Study Genesis 1-4

- God created women equal with men to work together to be fruitful and multiply, fill the earth and subdue it.
- Satan knew he was doomed, and his plan was to take with him those who God had created in His image.
- The desire of the Father is for men and women to walk together in unity, bringing the Kingdom of Heaven to earth!
- Jesus came to earth to show us the way.
- Your only need in this world is God's Word.
- God has made the way of escape through forgiveness.

CHAPTER 8

AND *God Said...*

"Where are you?"
GENESIS 3:9

God walked into Adam and Eve's shame and asked, "Where are you?" He called them out of hiding. He was not asking their physical location. He was asking, "Where are you in your spiritual relationship with Me?"

He still longs for a relationship with those created in His image, the masterpiece of all creation. He is still calling to us today, "Where are you?" *The choice is ours.*

This book is centered around three principles of life: the value of God's Word, the value of your words and the power of choice.

We must heed the words of Jesus' mother Mary, "Whatever He says to you, do it" (John 2:5).

I have tasted and seen that the Lord is good. Like many, I lived a miserable life and reaped the pain and heartache of trying to do it my way without submitting to God.

I am so thankful for the Holy Spirit, the One who continually woos and walks alongside, just waiting for an open door to walk in and bring life to a starving heart.

God has given us a valuable treasure, the gift of words, and with this gift there is great responsibility. We must remember that God bridges the gap to us by using words, and we connect to Him in the same way.

I remember when I had been feeling alone and fighting to keep my joy. One day on a walk, I looked up and said, "God, You are in heaven and I am in earth. How do I connect with You?" I immediately heard, *"With your words."* Amazing! With my words I connect to God. I began to think about prayer, you must use your voice to make your request known to God. Entering His gates with thanksgiving and praise is all through the expression of our words. Yes, words are what connect us to God and to other people.

We have the power to shape our world and to influence others with the tongue, but as I look around and hear people speak, I wonder, *"Do we really get it?"*

It is time for us to be accountable for our words. For the spiritual, mental and emotional impact we set into motion with our words in our life, in our family and in others. As a new creation, born-again child of God, we have the ability to bless and release life!

We must understand it is not a "word" problem; it is a "heart" problem. "Out of the abundance of the heart the mouth speaks" "Let the words of my mouth and the meditation of my heart be acceptable in Your sight, O LORD, my strength and my Redeemer" (Psalm 19:14).

> WE MUST UNDERSTAND IT IS NOT A "WORD" PROBLEM; IT IS A "HEART" PROBLEM

As a child of God, you are a target for satan. You are a weapon of light in a dark world, and your enemy knows that you are a threat and will do anything to stop you. You cannot allow the pressure of circumstances to shape your prayer life. Our prayers need to be formed by heaven's promises. We must value God's words, and our words need to echo the sound of heaven. The Kingdom of Heaven is voice activated!

Everything we will ever need is hidden in His Word, and it is our place to search for the answer to life challenges as a hidden treasure. Proverbs 2:4-5 NLT tells us, "Search for them as you would for silver; seek them like hidden treasures. Then you will understand what it means to fear the LORD, and you will gain knowledge of God."

Ephesians 6:16-17 are two powerful verses we need to understand to walk in this dark world. "Above all, taking the shield of faith with which you will be able to quench all the fiery darts of the wicked one. And take the helmet of salvation, and the sword of the Spirit, which is the word of God."

God framed the world we live in with words we cannot see. (Hebrews 11:3) Abraham called those things that were not as though they were. (Romans 4:17) The Shunammite woman said, "It is well" when her son was dead. (2 Kings 4:23) We must do the same! We must learn the language of heaven, and we can only do that by meditating on the Word of God. When we speak what God's Word declares in heaven, it gives substance to our sword and creates the shield of faith stopping all the fiery darts of the enemy!

Hebrews 4:12 NLT says, "For the word of God is alive and powerful. It is sharper than the sharpest two-edged sword, cutting between soul and spirit, between joint and marrow. It exposes our innermost thoughts and desires." *The sword of God's Word will divide between our earthly motives and heaven's intent.*

Before the Garden of Eden was planted, we were planted in Him, Before Adam and Eve were put out of the Garden, we were securely hidden in Christ. Before we were sinners, God washed us white as snow! Ephesians 1:4 NLT tells us, "Even before he made the world, God loved us and chose us in Christ to be holy and without fault in his eyes."

> OUR LIVES HIDDEN IN CHRIST IS A MYSTERY THAT HE DESIRES TO UNVEIL TO THOSE WHO BELIEVE

Our lives hidden in Christ is a mystery that He desires to unveil to those who believe. He is our life, the light of the world and the One who changes us. "For in Him we live and move and have our being, as also some of your own poets have said, 'For we are also His offspring'" (Acts 17:28).

God knows us and understands our desires and need. He knew the risk He was taking in giving men the free will to make choices. As Jesus was preparing for His earthly ministry, He asked each disciple one thing, "Come, follow Me." He is still giving that invitation to men and women today. As the disciples who chose to follow Jesus, we must also choose who we will follow.

It is extremely easy to get caught up in the cares of this world and only by making a choice to follow God, intentionally seeking Him, can we have the connection with God that we want and need. Matthew 6:31-33 NLT gives us clear direction in finding our God connection. "So don't worry about these things, saying, 'What will we eat? What will we drink? What will we wear?' These things dominate the thoughts of unbelievers, but your heavenly Father already knows all your needs. Seek the Kingdom of God above all else, and live righteously, and he will give you everything you need."

Purpose in your heart to grow. I have found in my life I have to purpose to welcome the Holy Spirit daily, to practice forgiveness daily, to live a generous lifestyle and purpose to finish well! There are many distractions that seek our attention. Disappointment and discouragement are common distractions in this world that open the door to deception.

God longs to connect to us through simple means in our day-to-day living. When Jesus invites you to follow Him, He didn't give you a timetable or guarantee change overnight. He didn't promise you would never lose your temper or have a bad hair day with a total meltdown!

As we start living intentionally on purpose to know God and the power of His resurrection, His promises are to never leave us or forsake us. When you purpose to do the right thing, day by day, year by year, He will walk with you each step of the way, leading you to a life of joy and peace in the Holy Spirit.

When we make a choice to accept Christ as our Lord and Savior, the new birth, we welcome the Person of the Holy Spirit without measure. We have all the power of God we need to live on earth as a follower of Christ investing in eternity!

We must cultivate the habit of honoring the Word of God in our life. As you fill your heart with His Word, God's character will begin to form in your heart.

It will not come overnight, but incremental changes will take place, and you will notice a shift in the atmosphere and peace that passes all understanding will guide you through life! Not because you never have another problem, but because you know He is in the problem with you and has made the way of escape.

Again, we see it is your choice!

The same question God asked Adam and Eve in the Garden, He is asking you today, *"Where are you?"*

> *"Today I have given you the choice between life*
> *and death, between blessings and curses.*
> *Now I call on heaven and earth to witness the*
> *choice you make. Oh, that you would choose life,*
> *so that you and your descendants might live!"*
> DEUTERONOMY 30:19 NLT

POINTS TO PONDER

Meditate on Isaiah 55:8-13

- Give yourself the gift of life, the Word of God, every morning starting each new day open to His Word. His ways are higher than ours.
- God still longs for a relationship with those created in His image, the masterpiece of all creation.
- This book is centered around three principles of life: the value of God's Word, the value of your words and the power of choice.
- God has given us a valuable treasure: the gift of words, and with this gift there is great responsibility.
- We have the power to shape our world and to influence others with the tongue.
- We must understand it is not a "word" problem; it is a "heart" problem.
- The sword of God's Word will divide between our earthly motives and heaven's intent.
- Purpose in your heart to grow.

CHAPTER 9

IN *Due* SEASON

"And let us not grow weary while doing good, for in due season we shall reap if we do not lose heart."
GALATIANS 6:9

Our walk in the Garden of our life takes a lifetime of learning and growing and will not stop until we are walking with the Master Gardener in His Garden of Life.

There is a season to plant, a season to cultivate the soil and a season of waiting for the "due" season to reap the harvest. Each season has a purpose. The waiting season is the most difficult for those who have put their total trust in God.

This is a season where character is formed. I have found during this season of my life, what God works in me is more important than what I am waiting for!

When we find ourselves in this season where we do not understand what is going on, we are in a place where we must diligently seek the help of the Holy Spirit. The Holy Spirit breathed a Scripture in my heart during a crisis in my life as I was hanging on for survival during the waiting season. Proverbs 20:24 NLT says, "The LORD directs our steps, *so why try to understand everything along the way?*"

This is constantly on my lips, "Lord, I don't understand, but since You are directing my steps, I will trust in You!"

You are stronger than you think. You are born again to overcome and walk in the Garden of your life fulfilling the dreams and visions God has placed within you in "due season."

As you walk the runway of life, remember what we learned from Eve; above all else, value the Word of God, understand the power of yours words and you have been given the power of choice!

I leave you with an encouraging Word from Hebrews 12. After sharing the great men and women of God in Hebrews 11 and the great exploits they had accomplished "with" the Lord their God, I find Hebrews 12 a great encouragement in my life:

HEBREWS 12
THE PASSION TRANSLATION

As for us, we have all of these great witnesses who encircle us like clouds. So we must let go of every wound that has pierced us and the sin we so easily fall into. Then we will be able to run life's marathon race with passion and determination, for the path has been already marked out before us.

We look away from the natural realm and we fasten our gaze onto Jesus who birthed faith within us and who leads us forward into faith's perfection. His example is this: Because his heart was focused on the joy of knowing that you would be his, he endured the agony of the cross and conquered its humiliation, and now sits exalted at the right hand of the throne of God!

So consider carefully how Jesus faced such intense opposition from sinners who opposed their own souls, so that you won't become worn down and cave in under life's pressures. After all, you have not yet reached the point of sweating blood in your opposition to sin. And have you forgotten his encouraging words spoken to you as his children? He said:

"My child, don't underestimate the value of the discipline and training of the Lord God, or get depressed when he has to correct you.

*For the Lord's training of your life is
the evidence of his faithful love.
And when he draws you to himself, it
proves you are his delightful child."*

Fully embrace God's correction as part of your training, for he is doing what any loving father does for his children. For who has ever heard of a child who never had to be corrected? We all should welcome God's discipline as the validation of authentic sonship. For if we have never once endured his correction it only proves we are strangers and not sons.

And isn't it true that we respect our earthly fathers even though they corrected and disciplined us? Then we should demonstrate an even greater respect for God, our spiritual Father, as we submit to his life-giving discipline. Our parents corrected us for the short time of our childhood as it seemed good to them. But God corrects us throughout our lives for our own good, giving us an invitation to share his holiness.

Now all discipline seems to be more pain than pleasure at the time, yet later it will produce a transformation of character, bringing a harvest of righteousness and peace to those who yield to it.

*So be made strong even in your weakness by
lifting up your tired hands in prayer and worship.
And strengthen your weak knees, for as you
keep walking forward on God's paths all your
stumbling ways will be divinely healed!*

*In every relationship be swift to choose peace over
competition, and run swiftly toward holiness, for
those who are not holy will not see the Lord. Watch
over each other to make sure that no one misses the
revelation of God's grace. And make sure no one lives
with a root of bitterness sprouting within them which
will only cause trouble and poison the hearts of many.*

*Be careful that no one among you lives in immorality,
becoming careless about God's blessings, like Esau
who traded away his rights as the firstborn for
a simple meal. And we know that later on when
he wanted to inherit his father's blessing, he was
turned away, even though he begged for it with
bitter tears, for it was too late then to repent.*

ENTERING INTO GOD'S PRESENCE

*For we are not coming, as Moses did, to a physical
mountain with its burning fire, thick clouds of darkness
and gloom, and with a raging whirlwind. We are not
those who are being warned by the jarring blast of a
trumpet and the thundering voice; the fearful voice*

that they begged to be silenced. They couldn't handle God's command that said, "If so much as an animal approaches the mountain it is to be stoned to death!"

The astounding phenomena Moses witnessed caused him to shudder with fear and he could only say, "I am trembling in terror!"

By contrast, we have already come near to God in a totally different realm, the Zion-realm, for we have entered the city of the Living God, which is the New Jerusalem in heaven! We have joined the festal gathering of myriads of angels in their joyous celebration!

And as members of the church of the Firstborn all our names have been legally registered as citizens of heaven! And we have come before God who judges all, and who lives among the spirits of the righteous who have been made perfect in his eyes!

And we have come to Jesus who established a new covenant with his blood sprinkled upon the mercy seat; blood that continues to speak from heaven, "forgiveness," a better message than Abel's blood that cries from the earth, "justice."

Make very sure that you never refuse to listen to God when he speaks! For the God who spoke on earth from Sinai is the same God who now speaks from heaven. Those who heard him speak his living Word on earth found nowhere to hide, so what chance is there for us to escape if we turn our backs on God and refuse to hear his warnings as he speaks from heaven?

The earth was rocked at the sound of his voice from the mountain, but now he has promised, "Once and for all I will not only shake the systems of the world, but also the unseen powers in the heavenly realm!"

Now this phrase "once and for all" clearly indicates the final removal of things that are shaking, that is, the old order, so only what is unshakeable will remain. Since we are receiving our rights to an unshakeable kingdom, we should be extremely thankful and offer God the purest worship that delights his heart as we lay down our lives in absolute surrender, filled with awe. For our God is a holy, devouring fire!

AMEN

For everything there is a season,
a time for every activity under heaven.
ECCLESIASTES 3:1, NLT

ABOUT THE AUTHOR

MEET *Joyce Tilney*

Joyce is a wife, mother, grandmother, author, and founder of Women of God Ministries. Her years in ministry have taken her throughout Europe, Asia, and the US with the message of "teaching women today from women of yesterday". Through personal examples and Biblical principles women learn practical how to's to overcome daily life challenges.

Joyce and her husband, Bill lived in Scotland twelve years, Women of God Ministries, was birthed during this time when the Lord spoke to her heart, "teach women today from women of yesterday."

After returning to the United States, the Lord spoke to her heart, "the printed word goes beyond your voice." She has authored six books and is a contributor to *Charisma Online Magazine*.

Bill and Joyce are members of Harvest International Ministry under the leadership of Dr. Che Ahn.

Joyce is honored to hear from her readers. To contact her:

JOYCETILNEY.COM
woman20-eve@yahoo.com

RESOURCES

Here are some resources for your spiritual growth. All books are available on Amazon in print and kindle. Visit joycetilney.com to learn more.

LEAH—THE SUBSTITUTE BRIDE

Unsought, undesired, and unloved, this was the story of Leah's life. She understood the pain of life. As she learned to cry out to God for help, she overcame the trials of life and fulfilled her purpose in life. Life is full of pain, but misery is optional for the Woman of God.

JOCHEBED—A MOTHER'S DECISION THAT SAVED A NATION

Most Christians don't even know who she is. The mother of three leaders; Moses, Miriam and Aaron. Her life speaks through her children. Listed in the "Heroes of Faith" in Hebrews 11, she was known by God. As a mother you have the opportunities to mold minds, nurture growth and develop potential like no one else!

THE REAL WOMAN—GROWS ROSES FROM THE THORNS OF LIFE

As we learn to use the hurt and heartache, *the thorns of life,* our heart is transformed into a beautiful treasure of hope. Buds of life will spring forth as you receive the truths of the life-giving revelation in this book, producing roses of peace and joy. *Life is full of pain, but misery is optional to the Woman of God.*

WHY DIETS DON'T WORK— FOOD IS NOT THE PROBLEM

This is not another diet plan, it is a battle plan! We are in a crisis when it comes to our health and well-being-spiritually, emotionally and physically. You don't have to be a slave to your body and emotions. When I submitted my food addiction to the Lord, He gave me a battle plan that worked from the inside out and took 90 pounds from my body!

The book and workbook are excellent for group Bible Studies!

FUEL FOR THE FIRE—MAN'S INSECURITIES ... THE DEVIL'S SECURITY

Living a Godly life in an ungodly world is not an easy assignment. Faith in God's Word offers us stability in life's every day journey and its unplanned detours.

As we become established in the Word of God, abounding in thanksgiving, the enemies lies are exposed, and we overcome the insecurities in our lives that hold us in bondage.

ALL BOOKS ARE AVAILABLE ON AMAZON IN PAPERBACK AND KINDLE.

For information about the books or ministry contact Joyce at: woman20-eve@yahoo.com.

JOYCETILNEY.COM

Only those that can see the invisible,
Can do the impossible!

www.ingramcontent.com/pod-product-compliance
Lightning Source LLC
Chambersburg PA
CBHW071306040426
42444CB00009B/1898